Looking for Invisible Clues

by Lee-Ann Wright

T0351208

What are invisible clues?

When someone has committed a crime, they usually leave clues. Many clues are **invisible** to an ordinary person. But a single fingerprint, a tiny piece of clothing, or a speck of mud can be 'invisible clues' that help expert **investigators** to track down a **suspect**. These sorts of clues can show that a suspect was at a certain place, and they can be used to help to solve a crime.

Collecting and examining these clues, and using them as **evidence** to solve a crime, is known as forensic science or forensics.

A fibre seen under a microscope

A speck of mud being collected

A fingerprint

CRIME SC

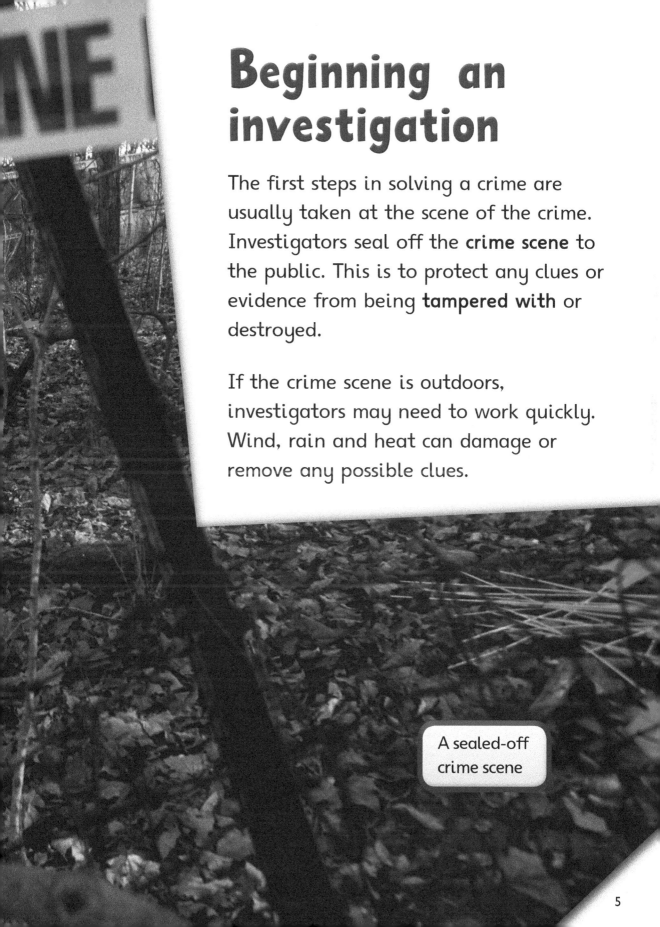

Beginning an investigation

The first steps in solving a crime are usually taken at the scene of the crime. Investigators seal off the **crime scene** to the public. This is to protect any clues or evidence from being **tampered with** or destroyed.

If the crime scene is outdoors, investigators may need to work quickly. Wind, rain and heat can damage or remove any possible clues.

A sealed-off crime scene

Different sorts of evidence

Investigators take many photographs at the scene of a crime – close-ups, from a distance, and from every angle. They draw diagrams and make notes of what they see and also make notes of what they think may be missing. Sometimes, they make video recordings, too.

All this is done in order to record the crime scene as they found it. The investigators mark the exact spot where things are found. The clues they find at the crime scene may be the only **proof** they have that will help to **identify**, catch and convict a suspect.

Sketch of a crime scene

Checking a crime scene very carefully

CASE 10-789-96
32 CENTRE ST.
OCTOBER 6

INVESTIGATOR:
SGT L. DUFFY

BOOKCASE

4M

COUCH

TABLE

BROKEN WINDOW

BOOKCASE

SAFE

TABLE

BOOKCASE

4M

A SCREWDRIVER   C BROKEN GLASS
B BRICK   D SAFE BROKEN INTO

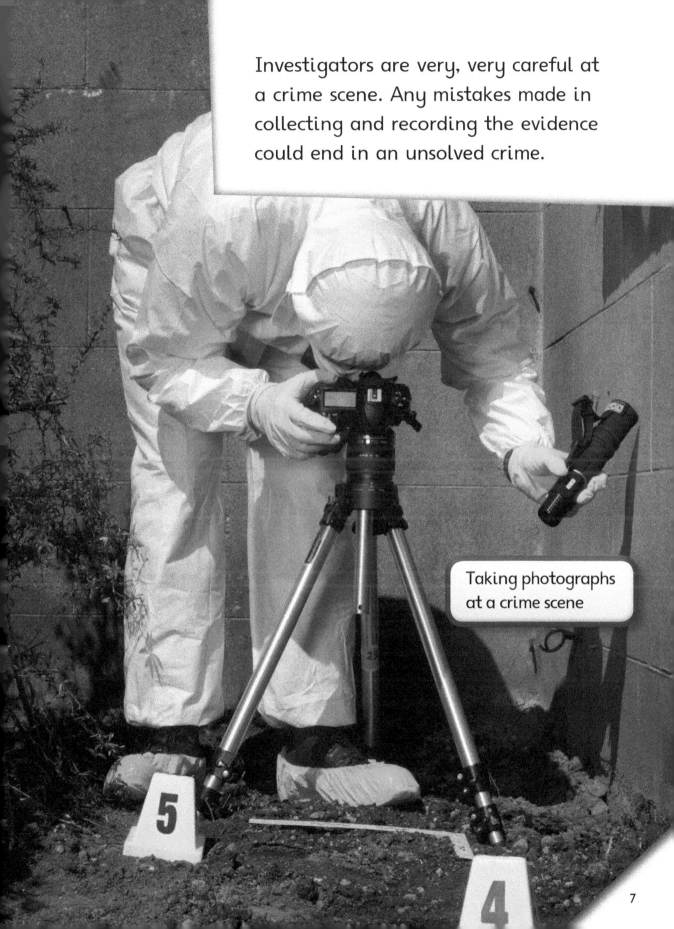

Investigators are very, very careful at a crime scene. Any mistakes made in collecting and recording the evidence could end in an unsolved crime.

Taking photographs at a crime scene

Trace evidence

Investigators know where and how to search for clues that will be used as evidence against a suspect. Even tiny clues will help. These tiny clues are called trace evidence. Some trace evidence is easy to spot. Some is not!

Examples of trace evidence can be an eyelash, a small piece of glass, or even dry **saliva** on a drinking straw.

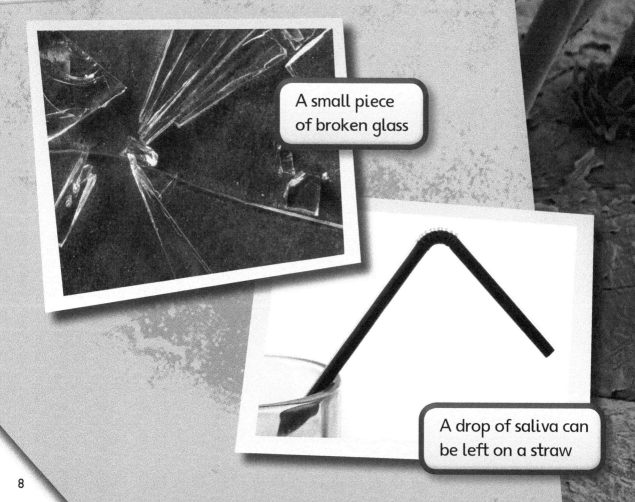

A small piece of broken glass

A drop of saliva can be left on a straw

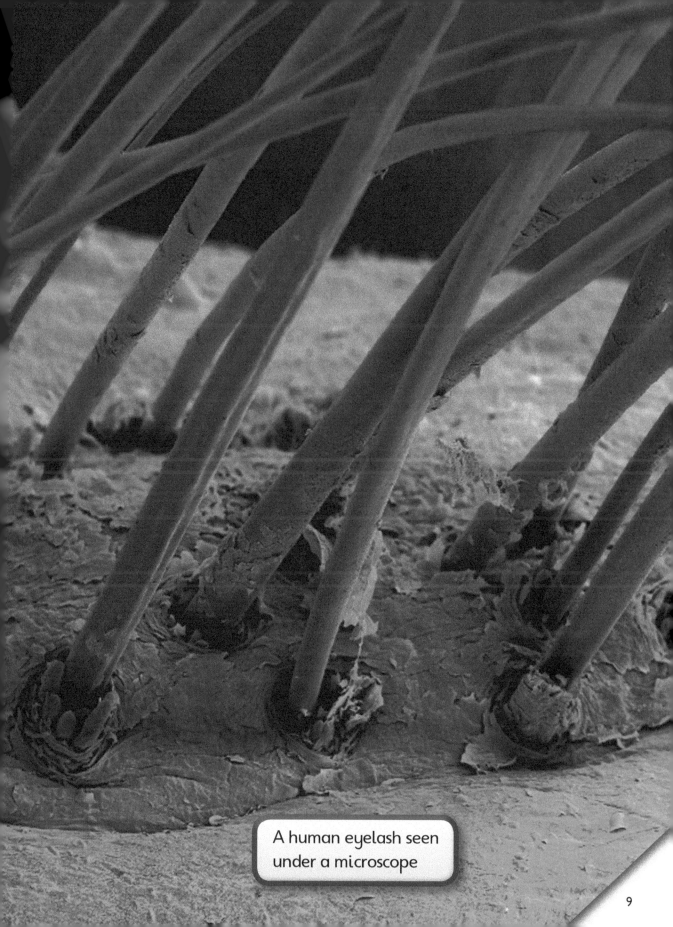

A human eyelash seen under a microscope

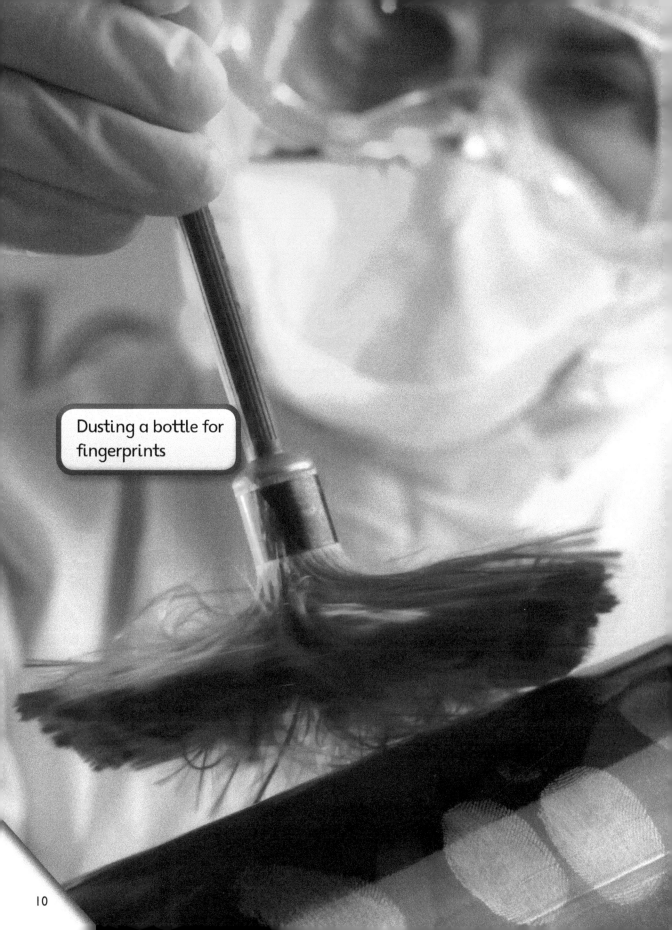

Dusting a bottle for fingerprints

Fingerprints

Fingerprints are one of the most important types of evidence that can be found at a crime scene. Investigators always wear gloves and are careful not to touch or move anything unless they have to as fingerprints can easily be smudged or wiped away.

Investigators search the crime scene for any easily seen fingerprints. They photograph the prints and make notes about exactly where they were found. They also search for anything that may have been touched or moved, or that looks out of place. Any of these could **reveal** a hidden fingerprint.

Our fingers are made up of many patterns of folds and creases called ridges. When we touch something, the oils and sweat in these ridges leave behind a fingerprint.

Impression evidence

A tyre track or shoe print is called **impression** evidence. This type of evidence can give investigators important information about a suspect.

For example, shoe prints can tell the investigators the size and weight of a suspect. They can also show if the person was walking or running. A tyre print can be tracked to the vehicle that left it.

If the crime scene is outdoors, investigators may need to put up a shelter, as impression evidence is easily washed away.

A tyre track

A police shelter at a crime scene

A shoe print

Collecting and recording evidence

Investigators may use tweezers, sticky tape, or a **scalpel** to collect trace evidence. Sometimes, they may use a special vacuum cleaner to pick up evidence that is too small to be identified.

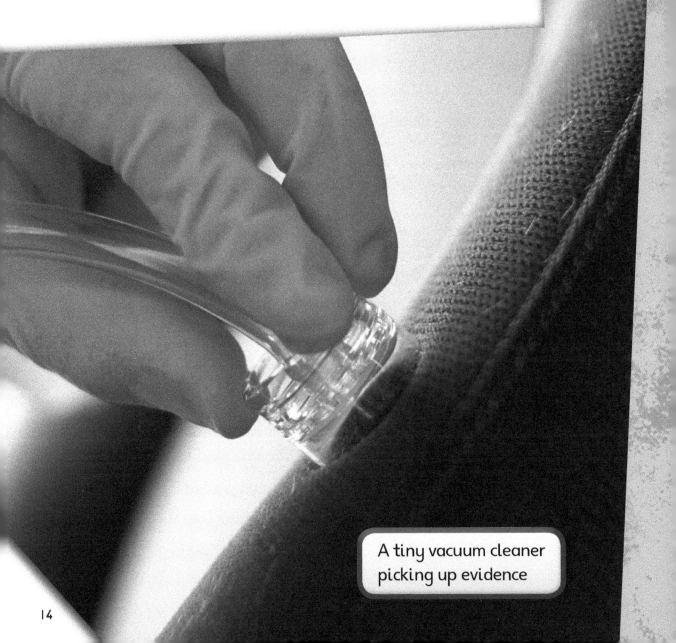

A tiny vacuum cleaner picking up evidence

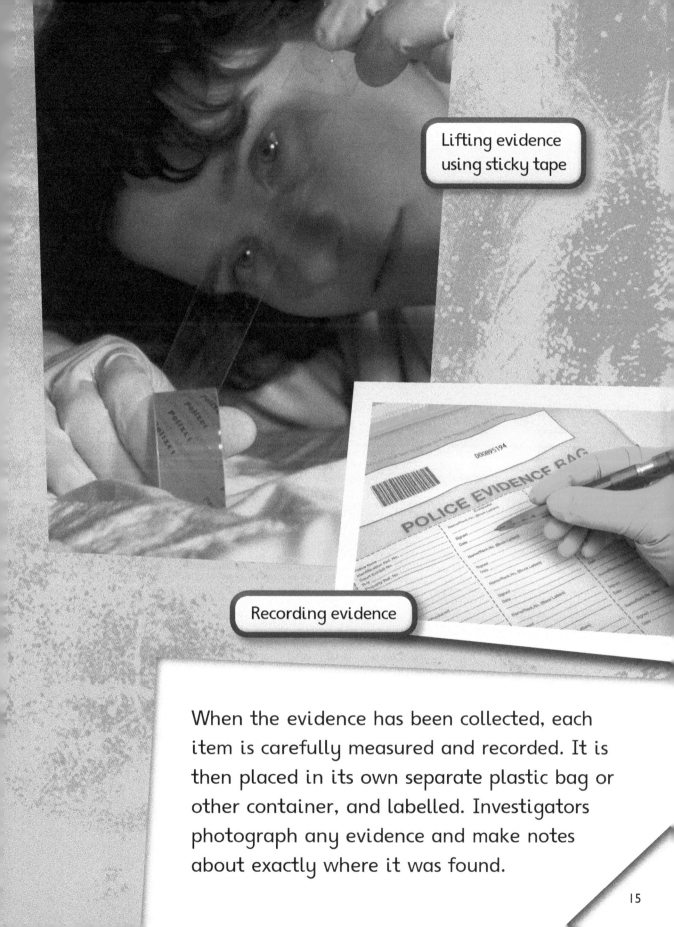

Lifting evidence using sticky tape

Recording evidence

When the evidence has been collected, each item is carefully measured and recorded. It is then placed in its own separate plastic bag or other container, and labelled. Investigators photograph any evidence and make notes about exactly where it was found.

Revealing fingerprints

Different types of powders and brushes can be used to reveal fingerprints.

Investigators dab the tip of the brush into a fine powder and gently dust a small amount onto any surfaces that may have been touched. The powder sticks to any fingerprints. Investigators keep brushing with more powder until the patterns of the fingerprint can be seen. They photograph the prints and cover them with a piece of transparent sticky tape. The tape can also be used to lift the fingerprints from the surface.

Using powder to dust for prints

The tools needed to lift and record fingerprints

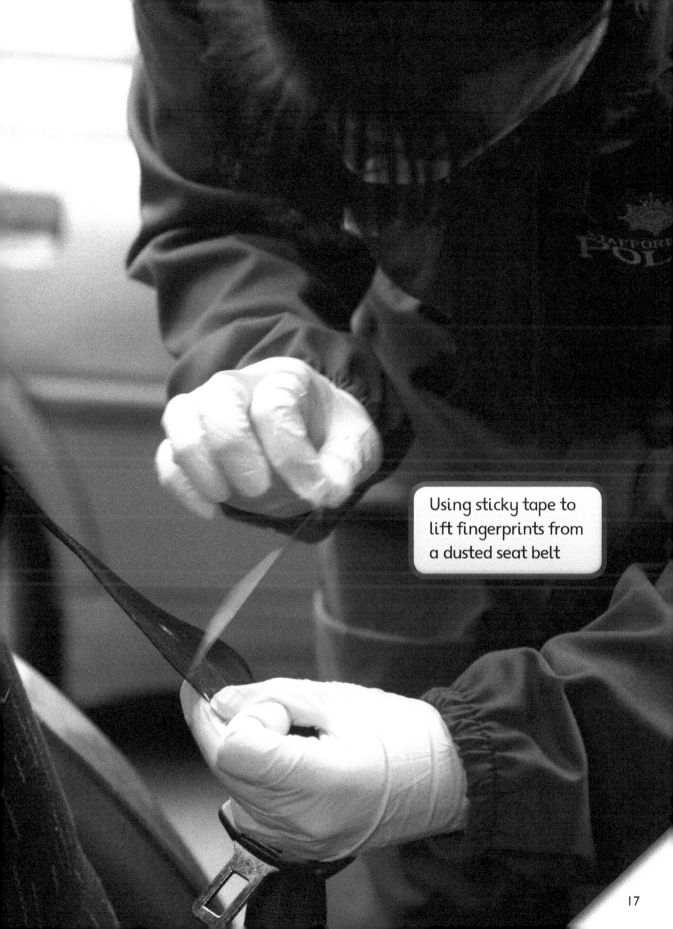

Using sticky tape to lift fingerprints from a dusted seat belt

Using superglue

Investigators often use the superglue method to reveal fingerprints. This method of revealing prints does not destroy a faint fingerprint in the way that brushing with powders can.

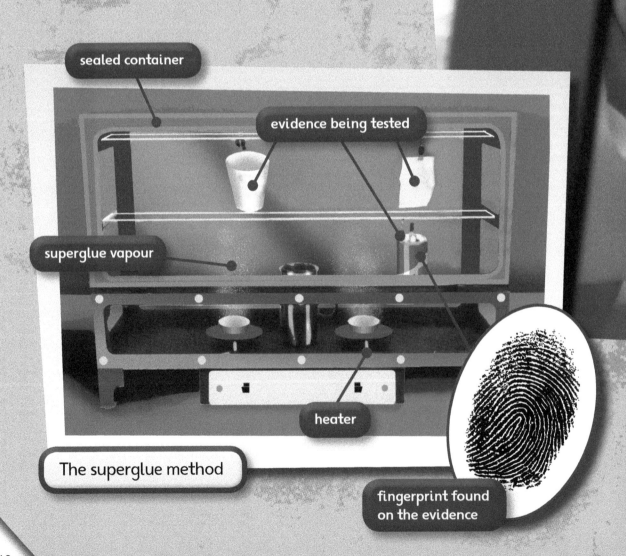

sealed container

evidence being tested

superglue vapour

heater

The superglue method

fingerprint found on the evidence

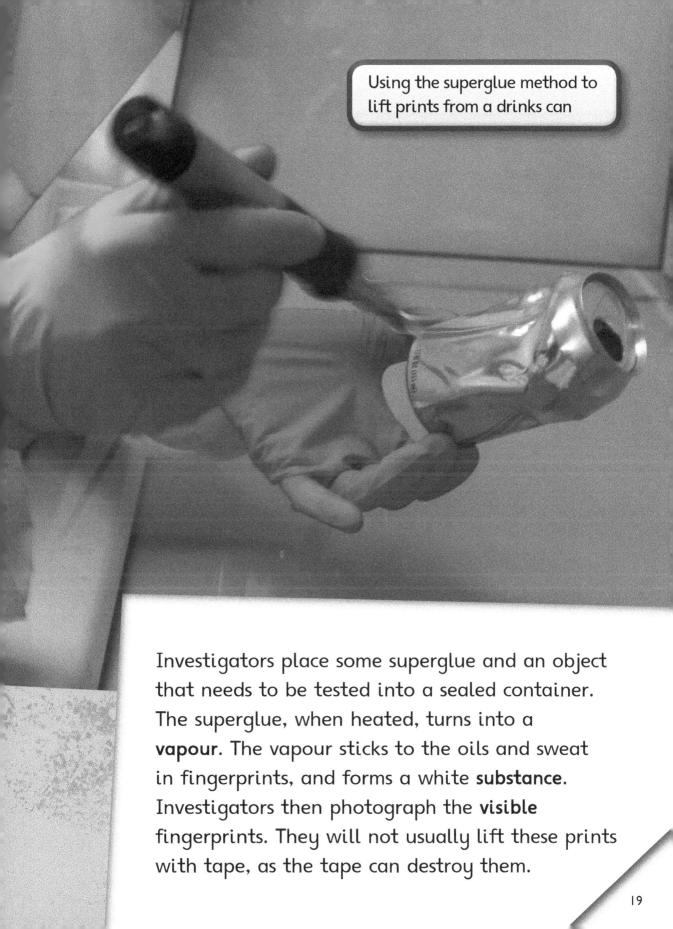

Using the superglue method to lift prints from a drinks can

Investigators place some superglue and an object that needs to be tested into a sealed container. The superglue, when heated, turns into a **vapour**. The vapour sticks to the oils and sweat in fingerprints, and forms a white **substance**. Investigators then photograph the **visible** fingerprints. They will not usually lift these prints with tape, as the tape can destroy them.

Tracks and prints

Tyre prints and shoe prints can be found in mud, snow, sand and soil.

First, the investigators photograph the impression. They then remove any twigs or leaves lying loosely on top of it. A metal frame is placed around the impression. The impression is then sprayed with a special spray. This helps to harden any loose dust or dirt.

An impression made by a shoe print

Pouring the powder and water mix into the frame

A powder is mixed with water. Investigators gently pour the mixture onto the impression. When the mixture has dried completely, the investigators can lift a cast of the impression.

The cast

Checking fingerprints at the laboratory

At the laboratory

Once all the evidence at the crime scene has been collected, measured, recorded, sealed and labelled, the investigators send it to a crime **laboratory** for **analysis**.

While the police **interrogate** witnesses and possible suspects, the investigators carry out tests on the items of evidence from the crime scene, and on samples taken from suspects. They use specially made scientific equipment, including different sorts of microscopes, to look at samples in great detail.

A computer scan of a fingerprint. The red dots show the investigator where to compare the print with another print

Analysing fingerprints

Analysing fingerprints can be an exact method of identifying a suspect. A computer can very quickly compare one set of unidentified prints against a file of around half a million prints. It comes up with a list of prints that closely match the ones from the crime scene. A fingerprint expert then compares the prints and, hopefully, makes a match.

Comparing unidentified prints against a file of prints stored on a computer

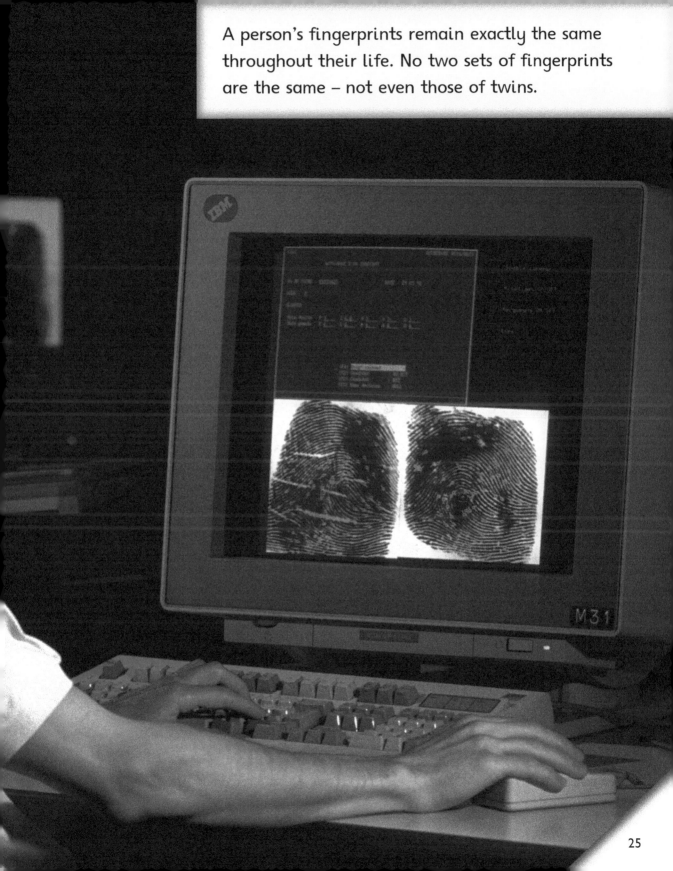

A person's fingerprints remain exactly the same throughout their life. No two sets of fingerprints are the same – not even those of twins.

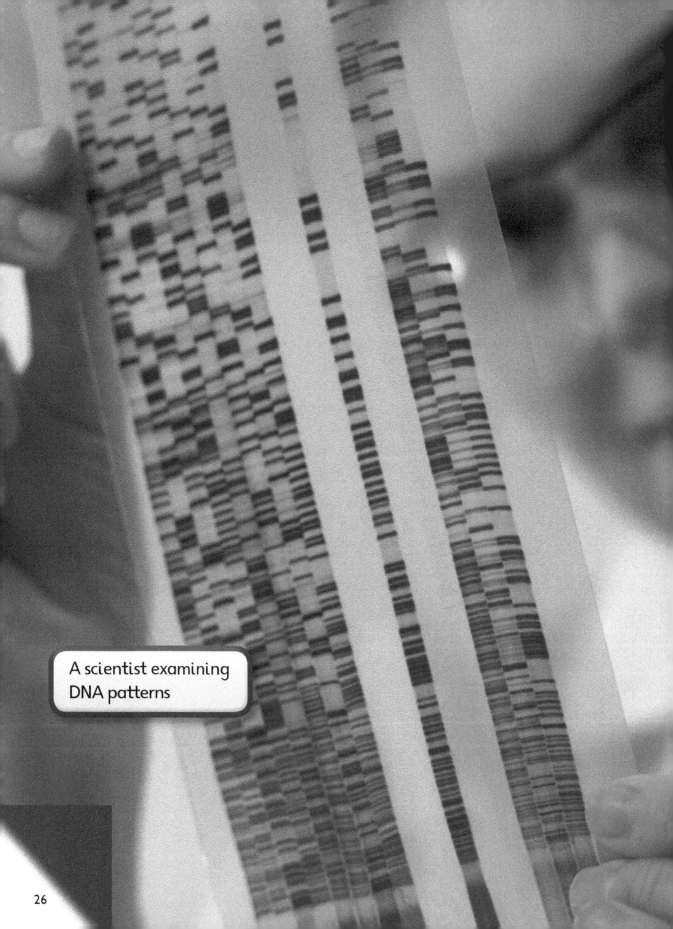

A scientist examining
DNA patterns

Analysing DNA

Forensic scientists can examine tiny **DNA** strands in hair or skin cells found at a crime scene. Each person's DNA is different from any other person's – except for identical twins.

Scientists use a method that makes copies of the tiny strands of DNA. As with fingerprints, a computer can compare the DNA against thousands of others stored on file. Once the computer comes up with a match, the scientist will check them carefully and come to a decision about a likely suspect.

DNA is a chemical material found in almost every cell of a human body.

Guilty or innocent?

Some forensic evidence is difficult and confusing to analyse, so different investigators might come to different conclusions. There is a lot of material for them to sort through, and they need to identify what is important, and what they can ignore.

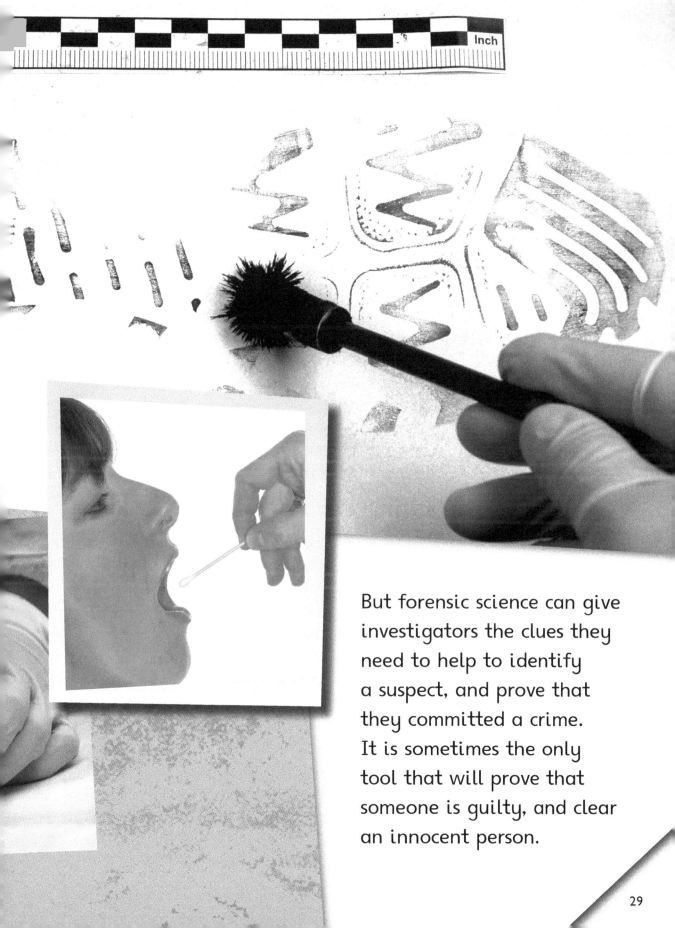

But forensic science can give investigators the clues they need to help to identify a suspect, and prove that they committed a crime. It is sometimes the only tool that will prove that someone is guilty, and clear an innocent person.

Quiz

1 What is an example of 'trace evidence'?

   a a footprint

   b a confession written on a piece of paper

   c a hair

2 Why do the police seal off the scene of a crime?

   a in case evidence is removed or tampered with

   b so that they have room to work

   c so that people can't come and watch

3 What is a suspect?

   a a witness

   b someone who may be guilty

   c an innocent person

4 What can a shoe print tell an investigator?

   a where the shoe was bought

   b the size and weight of the suspect

   c whether the suspect is male or female

Answers on page 31

Glossary

analysis	separating something into parts in order to study it
crime scene	where a crime has taken place
DNA	chemical material found in almost every cell in the human body
evidence	something that can help to prove someone has committed a crime
identify	be able to say who someone is
impression	mark made by pressing
interrogate	ask questions thoroughly for a long time
investigators	people who work to solve crimes
invisible	not possible to see
laboratory	place used for scientific testing
proof	something that shows that someone has committed a crime
reveal	show
saliva	liquid produced by glands in the mouth
scalpel	very sharp blade
substance	something that is made
suspect	someone who might be guilty
tampered with	damaged or changed
vapour	liquid or solid that becomes gas when heated
visible	possible to see

Index